the impossible.
What else is
worth doing?

Daniel N. Dunlop

Yes, you can do

A Human
Response to
Globalisation

Discovering
Associative Economics

A Human Response to Globalisation

Discovering Associative Economics

Marc Desaules

Translator: Christopher Houghton Budd

Associative Economics Institute
Canterbury, England / Neuchâtel, Switzerland

Published 2003
Associative Economics Institute
Canterbury, England / Neuchâtel, Switzerland
www.ae-institute.com

ISBN 0 948229 04 7

A catalogue record for this book is available from
the British Library

Printed by:
Cromwell Press, Trowbridge, England

Disclaimer

Offered in a spirit of on-going research, the publications of the Associative Economics Institute are intended to encourage awareness of associative economics and what this approach can mean for the development of an economic life that is truly in service to humanity. The views expressed in this publication belong nevertheless to their authors.

Acknowledgements

This book is based on more than twenty years experience of constituting, organising and financing various businesses, among which special mention should be made of L'Aubier near Neuchâtel in Switzerland. It also results from a collaboration with several colleagues, in particular Anita Grandjean and Christopher Houghton Budd, with whom the project of a guarantee mark for associatively-run organisations was developed (see appendix).

Gender

In this book, where reference is made to 'one' or to the human being, we have used the masculine. It might be politically correct to use constructions such as h/she, or to alternate gender on a random basis, as some academics now do, but this can look both awkward and ugly. It is also not clear that the charge of masculine domination really holds. It may be that tradition conceals an unspoken meaning, such as when one refers to the soul, or to a ship, for example, as she, rather than it. Moreover, outside of English, the use of gender is integral to many languages, so that the meaning behind its use may not be chauvinism but something quite different and even legitimate. It is perhaps important not to put a wrong emphasis on this matter, therefore. In any event, it is worth mentioning that those who drive change in the modern economic world, whether as consumers, investors or pathfinders, are preponderantly women.

Contents

Foreword

Economic life is not a necessary evil. On the contrary, it provides the ground for a conscious meeting with oneself and with others. And the difficulties one can encounter there are nothing but the secondary phenomena consequent on the awakening that economic life brings about.

As it appears to us today, the economy provides a measure for what we want to achieve consciously. Let things run on their own account and the economy will end up being experienced as repressive and confining. But put some consciousness into our actions, take things in hand, and economic life will lead us towards the most promising and encouraging horizons.

This book surveys recent economic evolution, beginning with a fresh look at the relationship between the economy and the human being, before going on to discuss the problems of globalisation and competition. It then considers afresh the axioms of economic science and describes how, to the extent they are able, the human being and his economic partners can work together fruitfully, and how fundamental to that is the role of money and its differentiation in modern accounting. The book ends with a perspective at once local and global.

Neither academic nor over technical, the approach chosen here may sometimes surprise. With a will turned resolutely towards practical life, it brings together certain general observations concerning human nature and the premises of economic science. It is both an introduction to associative economics and the starting point for a practical path belonging to today. And I dare to believe that its application will readily give rise to fruitful and very real consequences for economic life.

But first, a word concerning my references to Rudolf Steiner,[1] whose remarkable contribution to the analysis of modern economic phenomena[2] remains highly relevant even for

---

[1] Rudolf Steiner (1861-1925), Austrian philosopher, educator and economist.

[2] Rudolf Steiner, [1922]. *Economics*. New Economy Publications, Canterbury, 1996. Also important are *The Philosophy of Freedom* (1892) and *The Threefold Social Order* (1919), both available from Rudolf Steiner Press in England.

today. Like few other economists, he was able to describe the emergence of a world economy from out of national economies and he identified the need for new instruments of coherence and stability that are both institutional and monetary.

This book is the fruit of two decades of applied research undertaken with colleagues, which culminated in 1998 in the international registration of a Quality Guarantee Mark for associatively run organisations, and in 2002 in the establishment of an institute for research and training in associative economics, the Associative Economics Institute (see www.ae-institute.com). It is published at the same time as another work by my English colleague, Christopher Houghton Budd, that considers associative economics from the point of view of prevailing Anglo-Saxon orthodoxies.

The ideas I have shared here belong to ongoing research and do not claim to be final. In this spirit, all comments and suggestions are very welcome.

Marc Desaules
Montézillon, Neuchâtel, Switzerland
August 2003.

1 Where there's a will, there's a world

We live in a time when human life is increasingly conditioned by economic considerations. This fact has become even more marked during the last ten years with the ever more frenetic pace of globalisation. The future of the planet is in the control of fewer and fewer companies, to which even states submit themselves. An unforeseen bondage, is gripping humanity. Wherever, whether consciously or not, we invoke the creed of market economics, we are all pursuing the tendency to buy at the lowest price in the hope of faring better. Meanwhile, poverty goes on growing for billions of people, accompanied by an erosion of our natural, social and cultural environments. The stakes are high. The human being is touched to his innermost core, with human freedom in danger of being sold off cheaply.

There must be another way! Though everywhere the dominant concepts are *competition* and *market forces,* the challenge is to replace these words by *'association'* ³ and *responsibility,* and to use them to create the kind of economic landscape we will not be ashamed to pass on to future generations.

In the modern economy, the human being is reduced to the function of consumer. The credo of the market claims that it is enough for each to act in his self-interest; disparate acts will be managed by the market which – as if guided by an *'invisible hand'* ⁴ – will lead to the most favourable effects for society as a whole. This argument is simple and plausible, and therefore powerfully suggestive. But it invites what in French is called *'déresponsabilisation'* – human beings not taking responsibility for the consequences of their actions. It only calls on buyers to act for their own satisfaction

---

³ As used here, the term 'association' derives from Rudolf Steiner, who spoke of the need for economic life to be based on its own logic, which in a closed global economy necessitates human beings working together (associating) to meet one another's needs.

⁴ "[The human being] intends only his own gain, and is in this, as in many other cases, led by an invisible hand to promote an end which was no part of his intention." Adam Smith, [1776]. *An Inquiry into the Wealth of Nations.* OUP, World Classics, 1993, Book IV, Chapter ii, p.292.

by getting things as cheaply as possible. But thereby the market excludes from economic life the very essence of what it means to be human: to be unique and creative, endowed with free will, and capable of *'ethical individualism'*,[5] that is, of undertaking responsibility and of conceiving for every new situation the solution most suited to it. For market economics, the human being is seen as a disruptive element. This is a far cry from Denis de Rougemont's thinking and autonomous *'person'*.[6]

Market economics meets its limits today at the world level. Agriculture has become disoriented and is becoming lost in scandal upon scandal – all for the sake of producing mere ballast food at ever more derisory prices. Meanwhile, capital tries to multiply itself without connection to the world, and with no awareness that humanity is thereby becoming ever more sidelined. And everywhere increasing numbers of human beings are having to survive on less than a living wage, are becom-

---

[5] *The Philosophy of Freedom*, op. cit.

[6] Denis de Rougemont (1906-1985), Swiss writer and advocate of European federalism. Author of *The Future is within Us*, [1974]. Oxford/New York, Pergamon Press, 1983.

ing prisoners of the media, or are without direction in their lives.

The only conclusion we can draw from this is that competition does not result in the regulation expected of it. Quite the opposite!

Therefore, let us dare to strike a new path… Refuse the idea that competition can lead – even indirectly – to regulation of the economy; then place the human being at the heart of economic life. Although each time different and unique, we will then always have a clear and certain point of departure. For the human being is able not only to perceive in himself both his weaknesses and his potentials; he also has the ability to perceive other human beings and their needs. Let us then have the courage to believe that the best way of responding arises from the autonomy and freedom of the human being, *combined with responsibility*.

Even so, it is not a question of waiting until the human being becomes a better creature. We need a tool, an organ of perception, that will allow us to observe the world and to anticipate the consequences of our deeds. This will of itself engender a sense of responsibility. This tool exists but it is only very partially present: it is money, figures, and accounting.

18

One should not be afraid of their abstract and reductionist character. Just as the brain – an almost dead organ – enables the human being to form an image which allows him to become aware of himself, so the instrument of figures reveals the effects of human actions in the world. In the sense to be explained in the course of this book, money is the only thing able to reflect the values of goods and services in circulation. Thanks to this tool, we can all rise above the level of different personalities, languages and cultures. Thereby, too, the most diverse initiatives can work together. Because the world of figures is transparent, it dissipates doubts, makes competence objective, and underpins the taking of responsibility. It makes clear to us one another's needs and calls on us to answer them. The consciousness which this brings engenders creativity and the commitment of one's faculties in service to others.

This enables the whole economy to change its tone. Awareness of the problems of others leads to association, in the sense given earlier. Economic actors become responsible towards the world; prices become indicators rather than weapons. Human beings grow in stature.

Awakened by their contact with one another, they become responsible for their own future.

At this stage, the economy is no longer described in terms of inflation, unemployment, rates of interest, money emission, balance of payments, and speculation. These become secondary phenomena. Instead, economic life begins to reveal its true nature: reflecting the actions of the human being and enabling them to become coherent with those of others. In other words, economic life makes visible human destiny and provides a place for individuals to express themselves. At the same time, *qua* science it becomes accessible to everyone and is no longer left only to specialists.

2 Between agriculture and finance

The economy is a world that makes visible the exchanges between human beings when they meet one another's needs. It expresses itself in terms of values, which give rise to prices and thus figures as a reflection of the exchange of goods and services, contracts and other human relations.

The economy appears between two poles. The one pole is nature with all the occupations which are connected with it – such as agriculture.[7] The seasons' round determines all its tasks and governs its everyday life. All deeds connected to it strongly engage the will. In this intimate dialogue with nature, human activity takes on a deeper meaning; the forms, colours, flavours, and smells of its products keep us linked to the vast world of nature,

---

[7] Notwithstanding that industrialisation and developments such as genetic modification seek to wrest agriculture from its embeddedness in the natural world and prevent it from fulfilling its role in economic life.

even though in today's economy we give little value to such things…

The other pole is capital with the many activities it gives rise to – all of which touch on finance. Almost without engaging our will, just through our conscious presence and the intervention of our intelligence, capital gives rise to values which come and go, multiply, and are transformed. Everything here is directly value; but does it make sense?

All human economic activities take place somewhere between the two poles of meaning and value. Through the commitment and organisation of his labour, the human being is called on to create the balance. Everything depends, on the one hand, on the way that he manages to give a value, and thence a price, to the quality of goods, and, on the other, on how he makes sense of the financial world.

Just as light reveals the world to us between two limits, the infrared and the ultraviolet, so the economy makes perceptible a world of values in a domain bounded on the one side by nature and on the other by capital.[8] If we

---

[8] For an understanding of world economics, this image, from Steiner, is both precise and fecund. *Economics*, op. cit., Lecture 1.

go further in the direction of nature, we pass into the infrared and things stop having a value and stop being visible for the economy. Swallows, for example, may swirl all day long in the course of feeding and thus conform to the order of nature, but they are not part of economic life. The other extreme takes us into the ultraviolet and into capital movements and the laws which govern them. The risks of the stock-exchange and the mood swings of the secondary markets are as foreign to and invisible for the economy as the processes of nature. In this regard, we need to take care, therefore, not to transpose any laws discovered in connection with the movements of capital to the rest of the economy.

3 Win-win

The image of the economy as a world reflected in figures could easily lead to the belief that we should master the future by mere calculation. But here a phenomenon deserves particular attention, because it illustrates well how in economic life we need to learn to read through figures and not just make calculations and apply their result.

Too often, for example, we think that when a person sells something to someone else, one of them can only gain if the other loses. In brief, we think in terms of winners and losers! Yet nothing could be less true, as more attentive observation would clearly show. We need to realise that the values of things always express their relation to human beings, without whom nothing would have value. The price a man asks for an article, say 1 for an apple, indicates only the sum of money which he wishes to receive in exchange for his fruit. If he fixes the price at 1, it is because he attributes more value to his customer's money than to the apple. Now, when a buyer appears, he will only buy the apple if – and this is true of all transactions – he attributes more value to the fruit than to the money in his pocket. If, for him, the fruit has less value than 1 of money, he will not buy it! Thus, in any exchange (sale and purchase), both seller and buyer make a gain.

That we have come to believe there can only be a winner if there is a loser is not due to an economic phenomenon, but to a power relation that has entered in! If one party loses this is a matter of rights. Either one of the parties is deceived in the exchange, or there is use of force, resulting in theft. The feeling of injustice which is then felt confirms that it is indeed the sphere of rights that is at issue here. However shocking it can appear at first sight, this observation can be generalised: strictly speaking, injustice can never emanate from economic life![9]

---

[9] This is not an exaggeration. One would do well to look twice before attributing injustice to economic processes. Invariably, they have their origin in aggrieved rights. *Translator's note*: Reparation payments, for example, always tend to be set higher than is economically possible. A litigious society has a similar character, as do strikes. They represent grievances of the sense of right and cannot really be remedied by economics or money. The level of payment merely

Furthermore, as we have seen, after every exchange the total of all values is always greater than before. Every exchange is the source of an inevitable and inexhaustible surplus of value which has its origin in the diverse needs of human beings. By satisfying his own needs through exchange, the human being always creates more values than he needs. Nothing and nobody can change this. It is a phenomenon inherent to the economy, which not only puts a check on the Cartesian conception that nothing is created, nor anything lost, but obliges us to recognise that in economic life figures point to a dynamic arithmetic where $1 + 1$ inevitably make more than 2.

There, in the heart of the economy, such mysteries are so many winks of an eye, inviting everyone to take closer interest in this fascinating world…

---

marks the point at which the grievance is abandoned by the aggrieved party, the price to buy him off! Better, surely, not to engender grievances in the first place.

4 From mechanism to organism

What position does the economy occupy in society? To answer this question, let us look at social life as we would an organism with three autonomous systems and which owes its coherence to their continuous interaction and interpenetration.[10]

To think in terms of an organism with all its wondrous complexity, one has to abandon once and for all the idea of something mechanical. It also requires one to drop the idea of hierarchical centralisation directing all the phenomena involved. In its place, we need to consider several systems – independent in regard both to their constitutions and their functions – and to learn to perceive that they nevertheless achieve coherence. This implies more radical change of method than may appear at first sight; something whose importance we should not underestimate. The move

---

[10] *The Threefold Social Order*, op. cit.

from the mechanical to the organic world requires a change in the mode of observation and the adaptation of the scientific method to the laws of the living. This is a necessary step, however, and the only one that can lead to a fruitful image of social life.

This approach presupposes two preliminary stages. The first: the use of a model which can serve as a reference to guide this approach and to direct our understanding. In this book, this is the human organism. The second: the development of a sense for what is disease and what is health in an organism.[11]

Turning now to the human being. In the form of the body, on the one hand, we have a *head* system, protected by a peripheral bony structure, where the essential function takes place inside in the brain; on the other, a *limb* system, carried by long bones, where the activity takes place 'outside' in the muscles or in the metabolism. Between them, a *heart-and-lungs* system is maintained in a semi-protected, semi-open cage. The different natures and forms of these systems are further reflected in their functions and in the way they are linked

---

[11] This idea is developed in the next chapter.

to the world. The head system is the seat of consciousness, opening to the world by means of the senses. The limb system generates heat and life; its link with the environment is made through food and movement. The heart-and-lungs system maintains the rhythm for the whole body and is connected to the world by the breath. The purpose of these observations is to take as our model an organism, which, because we find it in our own constitutions, we can each experience directly and thus make real. It will then be possible to refer to it when turning to the social organism.

The social organism also has three systems. The first system, dealing with the satisfaction of human needs, is necessary if human beings are to manage their material connections with the world at large: this is the *economy*, corresponding to the head system in the human organism. Its domain comprises the particular resources of a region, and its tendency is to bring about trade on a worldwide scale, embracing the whole of humanity. The second system concerns all that can be called the *life of rights*, all that concerns the relations between human beings. Its domain is the state, understood here strictly as the sphere of law and politics, not as the nation-state, which is an agglomeration of all three spheres.[12] Its realm is that of a country and it is analogous to the heart-and-lungs system. The third system, *the cultural life*, comprises everything which becomes integrated into social life but emanates from the natural gifts, be they intellectual or manual, of every human being considered as an individual. This is comparable to the metabolic system of the human organism.

Although only partially in our consciousness, these three systems are linked to the three ideals which resounded for the first time – but possibly too soon in history – during the French revolution: *freedom, equality, brotherhood*. Freedom underlies cultural life and the manner in which the contribution of each human being to society should be organised. Equality underpins the rights life and the democratic

---

[12] The state as the body of rights life is not to be confused with the concept of the nation-state, introduced by Woodrow Wilson at the end of World War I, whereby a cultural identity is amalgamated with a legal constitution and a national economy. This has been the basis ever since of all new constitutions and declarations of independence and lies behind most of the murderous ethnic conflicts of the 20th century and is to this day the main obstacle to a healthy world economy.

way of managing relations between human beings. Finally, brotherhood is, or should be, the foundation of the economy. To the modern mind this last may be a surprising statement; even so, given the parlous conditions resulting from competition, it offers a ray of hope.

For anyone who wants to contribute in a constructive way to a social order favourable to the development of humanity, one of the great urgencies of our time is to learn to discern these three constituent systems of society, together with their distinct features and fields of application.

Head and nerves	Senses	Conscious (dead)	Economy *(satisfaction of human needs)*
Heart and lungs	Respiration	Rhythm	Rights and politics *(relations between human beings)*
Metabolism and limbs	Nutrition and movement	Unconscious (living)	Culture and education *(contributions from spiritual and manual faculties)*

Characteristics of the human and social organisms.

5 Pathogenesis and salutogenesis

To consider social life as an organism leads to the question of health and disease.

Health means equilibrium, which by definition is an unstable state. It is the 'game' of life to achieve organic stability by an ever-renewed conquest. It cannot therefore be a matter of miraculous remedies which provide cures for all time, just as there is no food which can satisfy one's hunger for ever.

In this domain, the conception which has dominated science for three hundred years is that of *pathogenesis* (from the Greek: origin of suffering). This approach tries to know and master the factors which bring disease. Thus, most modern medicine is determined by the question: What causes disease and how can it be eliminated? In contrast, a new kind of research investigates the causes of health and thus puts the emphasis on *salutogenesis* (from the Latin and Greek: origin of health). Since the 1960s[13], salutogenesis has sought to understand what favours health and cure. For example, in the case of an epidemic, it does not ask what virus is causing the illness, but why do some people avoid catching the disease? The central question here is the ability to strengthen the human being when faced with a vector of disease, a problem, or a source of stress. In brief, how to learn to transform imbalance into new balance.

In the social organism we cannot ignore these two approaches. We can, of course, identify several causes of the pathological tendencies which are leading economic life into a dead-end. But the devastating effects of today's economic pathologies are so widespread that we also have to look urgently at the foundations of salutogenesis in social life. How, in spite of all our errors and all our excesses, can we bring the social organism into balance? For this, however, we need to

---

[13] The founder of this approach was the American sociologist and doctor, Aaron Antonovsky (1923-1994), author of *Health, Stress and Coping*, 1985 and *Unravelling the Mystery of Health - How People Manage Stress and Stay Well*, 1988, both London, Jossey-Bass Publishers.

reconsider the role, foundations and potential of modern economic life.

6 Globalisation: a problem wrongly stated?

Globalisation is a typical phenomenon of the 20th century, albeit one that is often seen in a negative light. In several respects, however, it is a desirable development in the current evolution of humanity. The awareness we develop because we live on the same planet increases our sense of responsibility. The birth of the ecological and various other social movements which are connected with it is a clear proof of this. Similarly, a worldwide sense of solidarity is coming about in response to the disparities between regions and populations. Finally, the division of labour, specialisation, and international trade lead us out into the world as a whole, bringing in their train worldwide communication of information and between people. Each of us is becoming more and more aware that he belongs to one humanity and lives on the same earth.

Alongside this fact, since the end of the World War II, the decisions of world powers have set the basis of a new world order. Chief among these decisions are the agreements of Bretton Woods in 1944 and the first formulation of international treaties on tariffs and trade (GATT) in 1947. Then came the Uruguay Round, beginning in 1986 and leading eventually to the creation in Marrakesh of the World Trade Organisation (1994), with its inclusion of agriculture in the agreements of the GATT, as well as agreements on services (GATS) and intellectual property rights (TRIPS). In this way, the door was opened to a type of globalisation driven by economic interests.

But these global decisions have repercussions for the life of signatory countries and by extension all countries. It is the autonomy in regard to rights and obligations within these countries that is most affected, in particular the laws concerning the environment, conditions of employment, social security, and limitations on the movement of capital. The increasing power of the economy reduces rights to so many items for negotiation or indeed sale. The economy functions less and less in service to human beings, becoming instead the determinant of social life as a whole.

What is happening here?

First of all, by widening its horizons to those of the world as a whole and by clarifying new agreements as to its purpose and the scope of its activity, the economy is responding to our increasing sense that we comprise one humanity on one planet. This globalisation of the economy is a natural response to how best to meet everyone's needs. This is the true nature of economic life and in its proper sphere the gesture is welcome and consonant with the cosmopolitan spirit of our times. But this true nature is masked by two problems:

1. The prevailing economic order imposes on humanity the doctrine of unrestrained competition in markets. This is a major problem in many respects, because this doctrine is much less sound than it seems to be. Firstly, today's economics has little to no idea and not the slightest experience of an economy closed unto itself. Yet, the planet is a limited space and the world economy cannot but reflect this fact. Secondly, economics is based on an erroneous image of the human being that excludes the most essential part of human nature from its basic considerations. What

makes us human is what unfolds out of our individuality and not what results from our general inheritance. Because of this double negligence, economics needs to revisit its image of the human being, if, as a science, it wants to be up to the task of comprehending the world economy as a closed economy that includes, rather than marginalises, the human being.

2. If left unto itself, the worldwide tendency of the economy has a dangerous double side effect: on the one hand, it will lead to the globalisation of the rights life, which ought to be managed on a country-by-country basis, each according to its own lights; on the other, to a usurpation of the cultural life, which needs to be grounded in the individual human being.

Dangerous... because it is fundamentally foreign to every human being to allow his rights to be governed by too distant an authority, especially, a world authority. What arises as rights and obligations should only develop gradually in the context of human being to human being, because what arises as rights can only be truly accepted by human beings if they were party to their elaboration and able to comprehend the debate. Revulsion at the imposition of rights and obligations from the outside is at the base of all the feelings of minorities and revolutionary groups, with terrorism being only its most extreme and brutal expression. To globalise political life (rights life) is to head straight for disaster, the worst of all being the idea of a parliament raised to the level of the world as a whole and issuing world laws.[14] This path runs counter to the need to keep the rights life country-specific in order to facilitate the co-existence of different groups and cultures.

…and dangerous because it would be a prelude to the collective determination of the world of belief, of thinking and of self-expression – a sort of ban on thinking for oneself, a foretaste of which we already have in the manipulation of information by the media. We need the courage to see that that would mark the end of any humanity deserving of the name and open the door to a world, the like of which was already imagined by George Orwell more than half a century ago.

---

[14] George Monbiot, 2003. *The Age of Consent.* London, Flamingo.

To understand the problem of globalisation correctly, therefore, we need first to recognise its underlying *historical* justification, then to review the foundations of today's prevailing economic theory. Above all, we need to recognise the dangers inherent in globalising those aspects of society concerned with rights and the autonomy of the individual.

7 The limits of competition

In today's economic sense, competition is the race between two or more people, each of whom aspires to the same advantage and tries hard to win it for himself. Manufacturers and storekeepers alike, compete to produce or sell identical or similar goods at the lowest possible price. The *principle of unrestrained competition* is one of the bases of the current economic order. It aims to bring prices to the lowest level that it is possible to achieve. The regime that ensues from it brooks no intervention by the state that would limit the freedom of industry and business.

This approach is so fundamentally impressed on our minds today that one hardly dares to question it for fear of being branded a heretic or at least a naive dreamer. "And nevertheless it turns" – as Galileo is reputed to have said *sotto voce* when forced by the religious authorities of the time to renounce his discoveries on the movements of celestial bodies and the earth. Something of comparable dramatic intensity underlies today's situation in economics. The image we make of how the economy functions rests on an error of understanding, not to mention a lie, which denies the reality of the human being. It is this that gives competition so wide an influence. Even so, we cannot much longer maintain the illusion that unrestrained competition is the driving and regulating force of economic life.

Based on its etymology – from the Latin *competere,* to strive for something together with another, to pursue a common objective, to head towards the same purpose at the same time as others – competition has a nuance which is completely absent in its modern economic usage. The original meaning is thus linked to that of a game (that is, play), whether the simplest of children's ball-games or competition at the Olympic level. With play, however, we enter a world at a remove from ordinary reality. By definition, a game is never real. Otherwise it would no longer be a game!

In his *Letters on the Aesthetic Education of Man*, Schiller describes in a wonderful way how play is the mode of expression *par excellence* of what the human being bears within him as noble content. Here, the freedom of competition has its rightful place. Indeed, it is the interplay of individual personal freedom, in this sense, which makes for the cultural and civilising evolution of humanity.

But it is an error to let what is true for play slide over into economic reality, where human needs and world resources are at issue. Unrestrained competition is not valid where its effects are that people lose their dignity, starve, thirst, or suffer ill health… Equally not, when it touches the provision of water or air, the well-being of future generations, our genetic patrimony or the climate. This is *not* economics; it is theft, rape, war...

The erroneous basis of modern economics is compounded by the illusion of thinking that competition has a regulating role in the economy. Such a view can only derive from a very incomplete and biased observation of reality. When one focuses one's attention on a finished product or on a particular process, it is all too easy to regard the stimulation of competition as a source of efficiency. Often, however, something that can be true when considered close to, often ceases to have reality in the larger context. Competition leads to a myopic concentration on one isolated aspect, causing one to forget the rest of the economic process.

It ignores the natural environment, which somebody will have to care for one day; it ignores the social costs, along with all the ramifications of doing so; it ignores lost or damaged childhood due to premature specialisation; and it ignores the cost in terms of ill-health, or simply not having the time to live properly.

The inevitable tendency of competition is to lose sight of the whole. A gesture exactly opposite to any real meaning of economy!

We cannot one day but realise that, applied to economic life, competition is well and truly an error compounded by an illusion.

8 Land, labour, capital and money

Economic considerations usually begin by looking at three factors – land, labour and capital – the mutual influences of which give the basis to the whole economic life. However, each of these factors can become the point of departure for a claim on the proceeds of the economic process – claiming, here, that capital is the most important and therefore entitled to any surplus, there that labour is, and so on. Looking back in history, it is fascinating to see the ingenuity and the energy with which humanity has developed arguments in favour of the one or other point of view.

Today, it is by far capital that has the last word, but it is not the intention of this book to continue the discussion in these terms. On the contrary, the aim is to question directly the very discipline of economics precisely where it seems to get lost and to forget its own premises in its conclusions. Address this problem, and capital will of itself give to nature and the human being their rightful places in economic life.

To this end, let us ponder a little the role of money. From the beginning of its appearance in the economic process, from the first purchase or the first sale which it made possible, money has assumed an autonomy which is not economically desirable. Indeed, while the goods, the purchase or the sale of which it makes possible, wear out and lose their value, money, though only an intermediary, loses none of its. It thus becomes a disloyal partner in the economic process, and any economics worth its salt would take this into account by including suitably corrective action in its analysis of economic phenomena.

9 Axioms of an associative economy

It is one thing to describe what does not work and how it should work; and another to find a path that allows change to begin. So that discourse can become reality, we need to begin somewhere. Several possibilities are open to us.

We can set to work on projects based on different attitudes and alternative criteria. This is to change by doing, and at the micro level there are any number of such examples today, all deriving from such intentions, combined with immense commitment. Yet, in the world at large economic life continues on its disastrous path at a disconcerting speed.

We can gather together to draw attention to the glaring errors of prevailing economic doctrines and demonstrate opposition to their extension into all aspects of life. Challenging such forces can certainly be indispensable in countering the most urgent of our problems and has already been responsible for preventing several international economic agreements that fly in the face of human reality. For this we have civil society to thank. But to refuse the side effects of a system is never enough to prepare the basis of a future where human values can develop and blossom. Indeed, history offers many examples of revolutions which began with praiseworthy ideals, only to end in terror and bloodshed.

It is here that another path needs to open up by reconsidering the very basis of economic science itself. To question the foundations of economics may cause one to hesitate, but clearly economic science has taken a wrong turning. It has taken a road, along which the human being became lost to sight. And thereby economics lost its right to represent reality. Let us dare, therefore, to start again. After all, humanity has nothing more to lose.

All science rests on axioms, non-demonstrable propositions that are nevertheless convincing to the observation and common sense. So let us try to identify the first elements which, when recognised, can give coherence to economics, without requiring the exclusion of the human being as the main agent of economic life. It is not so much a matter of questioning the experiences of economics to date, but of beginning the necessary change of paradigm so that the human being continues to have a role in the play.

Firstly, we need to begin at the heart of economic thinking by reinstating the *human being* as such, possessed of a spirit and surrounded by nature. It is from human beings that economic life arises and human beings it should serve. Human beings have to remain the anchor point and cohering element of economic life. Because they have the potential to be free and autonomous actors, the bearers of initiative, decision-making and responsibility, they should be placed centre-stage. With the human being, we have a centre, capable of egoism, of course, but also – and it is precisely this that is all too easily forgotten – capable of enlarging their egoism to perceive the needs of others and to want to respond to them.

But we need to create around him the conditions that enable egoism to give way to ethical individualism[15] and allow the human being to assume the responsibility that goes

---

[15] See Chapter 1.

hand-in-hand with freedom – for it is the notion of freedom without responsibility that lies at the root of today's many economic ills.

This first aspect has also to consider the legal garment needed to clothe the initiatives human beings take. The form of this garment has such an important influence on its wearer that it is essential to analyze to what extent it favours or hinders human nature.

Secondly, we cannot avoid taking *others* into account. Whatever the economic context, as the source of will and initiative the human being is never alone. He is inevitably surrounded by *other people* with or for whom he becomes active. They form a periphery which comes to meet his initiative and intention; from them he receives an echo enabling him to perceive the consequence of his acts and their effects in society generally. It is essential, therefore, for the initiative-taker to meet with those who are for him a periphery.

Thirdly, however, no such meeting can take place in a way that is fruitful for the conduct of economic relations unless it is consciously guided by and conducted in a language that everyone can speak, a language, moreover, that is specific to economic life. Collaboration cannot happen if there is not the means to understand one another and if that means is not apt to the task at hand. This medium – at once a common language and an instrument capable of reflecting the values (and thus the prices) of the goods and services circulating in the world – is *money or accounting*.

These three elements – the human being, his economic partners, and money or accounting as the medium for their meeting – are essential for any science of the economy which begins with the human being. None of them can be ignored except at the risk of losing the human being also.

Just as, for Goethe,[16] colours arise only in the presence of light, of darkness, and of a medium which allows their meeting, so an associative economy begins to arise through

---

[16] Johann Wolfgang von Goethe (1749-1832), 1810. *Theory of Colours*. MIT Press, 1970. In his scientific work, Goethe stood opposed to Newton. Goethe constructed a science based directly on phenomena, those being the foundations of a mathematics of phenomena. Where Newton invented inaccessible processes, hidden behind the phenomena and therefore only verifiable in their effects, Goethe gave a comprehensive and verifiable explanation without leaving the world of phenomena. Goethe continues to be misunderstood today, but his contribution to science is nonetheless exemplary.

bringing together the human being as the actor (light), his economic partners (darkness), and money or accounting as the medium of their meeting. Just as, in this regard, Newton, inattentive to the role of darkness, misread light by defining it as the sum of colours, so Adam Smith, by not recognising the role of economic partners, discarded the human being as the key element in economic life, inventing in his place the invisible hand and competition in the market place.[17]

---

[17] Believing that human beings only collaborated to achieve monopoly, Smith said, "Never can good management be universally established but in consequence of that free and universal competition which forces everybody to have recourse to it for the sake of self-defence." *The Wealth of Nations*, op. cit. Book I, Chapter XI, Part I.

10 Starting with the human being

The recent evolution of humanity has delivered the responsibility for economic life into the hands of every human being. If the opposite seems to be true, it is only because we have yet to realise how to assume this responsibility consciously. In their hearts, human beings everywhere are feeling this change and beginning to react against the domination of the economic sphere– witness the many demonstrations against globalisation.

Previously – only two or three centuries ago – the situation was completely different. The economy was then the affair of professional corporations. Before that, it was for a long time under the control of princes and cardinals. And if one casts one's mind's eye still further back, those responsible for managing economic life merge more and more with the spiritual and religious leaders of ancient civilisations.

This journey has a double signature characteristic of modern times. The moment humanity began to bear responsibility for managing its own affairs, and thus the future of the economy, it lost its ancient relation with the divine. The Italian Renaissance and the appearance of the natural sciences illustrate the immense change of consciousness that came about at this moment in history. Without this event, the freedom we so take for granted today is simply unthinkable. However, a second impulse also came about at that time which is even more far-reaching. The natural sciences turned so exclusively to the material world that they gave rise to a conception which, by excluding the divine aspect of the human being, came to regard him as only a higher animal. Worse: the cause and reason for human evolution became attributed to a ceaseless fight to survive! It was in this landscape that the new discipline of economics grew up – modelling itself on Darwinism. From then on, it is quite natural that economics, seeing only the animal aspect of the human being, should flood civilisation with such ideas as 'everyone for himself' and structure education in order 'to arm oneself for life'.

Instead of evolving towards a science for sharing the natural and human resources of the world's economy, economics became warlike.

These considerations bring us to the heart of the subject: to start with the human being is necessarily to start with the image we have of him and this, as we have seen, can be very different.

To understand the image used here, let us dare to begin with an experience, at once the most objective because everyone uses it every day and in the same way to refer to himself, and the most subjective because it concerns the innermost aspect of the human being: the *I*. It does not much matter what one understands by this term; this is not the occasion for a philosophic discussion. The *I* reveals itself through its will, its *I-ness* or egoism, ranging from *lower egoism*, to *higher egoism*. The first is reactive and spontaneous. With no other purpose than self-defence or self-assertion, it rests on instincts and receives its force from the unconscious depths of human nature. The second needs an intention, a motif which links the I to a certain ideal, enabling it to draw strength from its heightened sense of purpose? These capacities of *I-ness* can be seen pictured vertically passing from the unconscious lower region of instincts to the upper region of conscious motives.

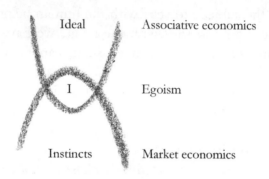

By widening the perspective a little, we can restate everything in terms of egoism capable of expanding itself to the dimension of a group or a wider idea, even the whole planet.

In economic life, the human being engenders very different effects depending on whether he acts according only to instincts or in the light of a precise and noble purpose.

If he leaves the choice of his behaviour to his subconscious nature, it is essentially the price of things and the way they are marketed that will matter. He then acts in the image of a

60

higher animal condemned to struggle for its existence. Like that of a sheep, his behaviour becomes predictable and the stuff of statistics, providing the justification for market economics and all that that name implies.

If, on the other hand, his behaviour is prompted by an awareness of people's needs and the necessities of a situation, he enters a space of freedom in which, in full knowledge of the facts, he is able to be responsible. His action is then truly human and can become the basis of an associative economy with all the potential that can result from the contributions of each and every human being.

Too good to be true? On the contrary! Based on the natural sciences, we have accepted an image of the human being which is far too narrow to be a match for the requirements of modern economic life. We must, therefore, see the human being in a new light so that we can become aware of and make room for the potential we all bear within.

It remains to see how we can give ourselves a legal framework suited to this task.

62

11 The birth of the legal person

It was an invention of the Romans to give the human being a quality of right, a legal reality. To the physical body, they added a body of right – from the Latin *persona*, the person; literally, a legal mask. To appreciate the importance of this development, we need to know that primitive legal systems made the physical body the basis of relations of right. A debtor who could not pay his debts was personally handed over to his creditor who could do with him what he wanted – sell him, reduce him to slavery, even kill him.

A sphere of rights then slowly developed, in recognition of such a person, conceived as having autonomy, but also rights and obligations. Under the influence of the Church, which refused the notion of a separate person, mask and masked became one: the physical person.[18] Emerging out of local traditions with

---

[18] The author of this development was Boethius (480-524 B.C.) who assimilated the person into the reasoning individ-

their different cultural or religious references, this went on to become the constitutional foundation of today's states.

However, this legal personality – 'body of right' – was not granted with the same precision to groupings of human beings, although some of them, such as the guilds or various professional corporations, reached considerable size. Through charters, they received, or gave themselves, rights and obligations. In this regard, the Church, with its orders, would have to be looked at specially.

A new stage began with the needs of large-scale companies. The explorer-entrepreneurs were animated by ideas for which they could not find sufficient financial means with a single monarch, so they looked for other ways. This was the origin of companies, such as the East India Companies and the South Sea Company. With the collapse of the latter, the question of responsibility reappears: cannot such a company also be recognised as a legal person able to assume responsibilities in its

---

ual being. This idea was taken further by Thomas Aquinas (1225-1274), eventually becoming accepted by the highest philosophical thought as well as passing into normal language.

own right, thus establishing a distinction between itself and its owners?

In ways that varied from country to country, the 19th century answered this expectation by gradually granting legal personality to such groupings. This marked the birth of today's companies (or corporations), foundations, and associations.[19] These new entities are real social beings. They can make decisions, act in their own name, and be charged with responsibilities. They are thus separately identifiable persons, in the same way that human beings are. Instead of a physical body, however, they have a body of statutes which details their name, their purpose, their organs, and their functioning.

What does all this mean? The human being became capable of creating a new realm of entities which, although enjoying the same rights as human beings, do not have the same spatial or temporal limitations. They have the possibility of spreading themselves over the entire planet and of lasting much longer than a human life. In this regard, they can outgrow

---

[19] In the UK in 1855; in Switzerland in 1883 for companies, 1902 for associations and foundations; in the USA in 1886, by way of a debatable interpretation.

the control of the rights life of the country which gave them their existence.

As a consequence, humanity now finds itself confronted by a new and immensely far-reaching challenge: Sorcerer's apprentice, we have put in the world a considerable number of beings that we did not imagine would become autonomous. And now we have to learn to educate and train them, so that they do not enslave us…

In this connection, the term for this in French is *'personne morale'*. In translating this book into English, however, 'moral person' seemed inappropriate, so the term 'abstract person' has been invented instead. For two millennia, the physical person and the rights sphere evolved together; then the abstract person appears. A completely new player in social life, it has to learn to live in society – a development that asks for a structure (set or 'body' of statutes) which allows the abstract person to maintain coherence between its freedom and its responsibilities, its decisions and its actions. What does this mean?

If the statutes of the abstract person merely aver to the personal instincts of the human beings who make up its organs (e.g. the Board or the General Meeting), it will be necessary to develop rights to protect society from the abstract person; and this should be a matter for each country to address as it sees fit. However, this is not so easy: because of the global tendency inherent in the economy, companies[20] are led to operate all over the world. In the conquest of such wide horizons they can acquire a power which they can abuse only too easily to manipulate the rights of any country to their advantage – a road that leads to the bleakest of perspectives…

But if the statutes of the abstract person call on the higher sensibility of the human beings who make up its organs, and on their awareness of its common aim, a 'self-education' of the abstract person will then become possible. This will allow it to become integrated into social life alongside physical persons (that is, human beings). Then we will see that, however 'abstract', this new player has also to be accepting of responsibility. In a world in which companies are increasingly acting on a basis of freedom *without* responsibility, this

---

[20] To mention the most widespread kind of entity for economic activity.

would open up a new path – one that is as
bright as the other is bleak.

12 Ltd, SA, Inc, AG: friend or foe?

By way of its structure and its organs, any legal form integrates the relationship between three essential elements: (a) those who carry an initiative and have a 'know-how' (entrepreneurs); (b) those, their partners, who recognise them, join with them and provide financing (investors); and (c) a common purpose or ideal.

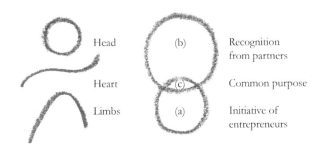

Physical person and 'abstract' person.

For the physical person, equilibrium depends on maintaining coherence between the limbs which act, the head which makes these actions conscious, and the heart which approves and finally assumes responsibility for them. When this is the case, the person will be truly human and his contribution to social life will be both desirable and fruitful. Otherwise, it will be necessary to distrust him, even to protect society from him. It is the same for an abstract person.

Let us look in particular at the limited company (or corporation),[21] because we shall see that this is probably the abstract person whose current form most approximates human nature. For better or worse!

For worse? We all know the disrepute that can attend modern companies. For better? No other form allows such an organic interrelationship between the entrepreneur and the investors, and all in the name of a common purpose. However, and this is true for all legal

---

[21] This is the name given to a company, in which the amount of capital is determined in advance and divided into shares, and in which liability is limited to the extent of one's investment. This form of abstract person can be found in most countries of the world, subject to minor differences due to local law and history. It is worth noting that in Switzerland it can also be explicitly set up for a purpose that is not commercial in nature, such as a philanthropic society.

forms, a main difficulty lies in the way power is integrated into the structure. It is here that the limited company is unique, because it permits of the greatest variety in this respect. This is what gives it its potential, but also, for many, makes it so troublesome.

To allow the best and avoid the worst is the role of a healthy structure. In terms of voting rights, this translates into the need to distinguish between the majority and the minority parties. Better put: how is the power to be neutralised in favour of the common purpose? Since power cannot be obviated, the point is to vest it such that it permits an activity to be led by those who initiate it and who are responsible for its successful existence. Of all legal forms, the limited company is perhaps the best suited to this task.

In any company, power belongs to capital, every share having the right to a vote. Normally thereby, the amount of power increases according to the amount of capital held, and this is the main argument made against the limited company by its detractors.

How can this be remedied?

One way is to allocate votes to people independently of their invested capital – giving to each investor only one vote. This is the basis of cooperatives. And yet, in answering the question this way, the cooperative – as an abstract person – goes from the frying pan into the fire: in avoiding submission to the provider of capital, it becomes dependent instead on the judgment of the greatest number of people.

As a side remark, we can note here that a similar problem arises in every membership-based society where, unless carefully structured, power can all too easily slide towards the members.[22]

The limited company can offer a solution to these problems because of the possibility it affords, for example, of creating preference shares such that the capitalisation can be structured so that the majority of votes are vested in a minimum of capital.[23] This majority can then be entrusted to an external organ,

---

[22] To find ways in which those carrying the initiative of an undertaking and those supporting it can meet without either using their power over the other, remains a challenge to modern law and, indeed, touches the larger question of the nature and evolution of modern democracy. To do justice to this topic, however, another book would be required.

[23] The way to do this varies from country to country, of course.

created especially for the purpose – for example, a foundation or a small association with an ideal aim – where the aim is to ensure the autonomy and perpetuity of the limited company.

Power is thereby separated both from the bearers of the initiative and from those who provide the financing. The meeting of the two can then become free and fruitful. Year upon year, the annual general meetings make this possible: (a) the entrepreneurs report on their activity, undertaken from the point of view association with close awareness of the business, but which they do not have the right to impose; (b) the investors become aware of the business's circumstances, but they have not the power to decide; and (c) the representative of the majority shareholder holds the ring, as it were, ratifying the proposals approved by the meeting.

What is otherwise an adversarial relationship and struggle for power becomes thereby transformed into a conversation between the entrepreneur and his investors, who then become joint partners in pursuit of a shared stated objective. By stilling the power, rather than wielding it, the entire dynamics of the company are changed, as, by extension, would be those of any economy which used this kind of company as its essential building block.

Many further aspects would need to be clarified to complete the image, but this description is enough to reveal the essential 'logic' of the idea and to allow one to sense its further perspectives. Transformed in its structure in the way described above, the limited company opens itself to a real 'self-education'. It is in this sense that it most closely resembles human nature, making it arguably the best partner for overcoming the problems we now face and build up, as abstract person among physical persons, a conscious economic future.

13 The story of money

Money and accounting evolved along with the development of consciousness and arithmetic.

The Chaldean and Sumerian civilisations from the 4th to the 2nd millennia BC – the oldest civilisations of which we have written traces (tablets of clay) – provide evidence of an accounting applied to the vast range of their economic activities, although at that time economic life was still wholly integrated with the activity of the temples.[24] Their narrative, an early form of *single-entry* book-keeping, consisted of recording chronologically and consecutively the movements of goods and cash, along with inventories taken at regular intervals.

We need to wait till the end of the Middle Ages, however – a time in Europe when most nobles issued their own currency (about fifty in France alone) – to find documents which

---

[24] Joseph-H. Vlaemminck, *The history and doctrines of accounting,* Paris, Dunod, 1956 (published in French).

show a new important stage: the introduction of a unit of account that operated independently of all other currencies in circulation. Equal to twenty shillings, the pound,[25] was the basis of a bookkeeping system that greatly favoured the Order of the Knights Templar.[26] In addition, the current account, one of their inventions, allowed one to keep a permanent balance. At this time, too, narrative gave way to the alignment of figures in columns.

Then, with the appearance of *double-entry* book-keeping, first described by Luca Pacioli,[27] the Italian Renaissance brought a novelty comparable to that of perspective in pictorial art. This contributed greatly to the development of the Italian economy, and then to that of the Netherlands. Its use then progres-

---

[25] The name deriving from one pound weight of silver.

[26] The Knights Templar was a religious-military order founded in Jerusalem in the 12th century, but brutally supressed by Philip the Fair in the early 14th century. In certain respects, they were the forerunners of modern banking.

[27] Luca Pacioli (1445-1510), Italian mathematician and Franciscan monk, author of the « Summa » in Venice in 1494. A friend of Piero della Francesca, Leonardo da Vinci, Ludovic Sforza, and Pope Leo X, he is considered today as one of the great scientists of the 15th century.

76

sively, but only gradually, extends over the rest of Europe. By then also Roman numerals had given way to Arabic. We thus arrived at the form that accounting has today.

Then with the 19th century came the beginning of the separation of money from accounting. Having evolved together up to that point – the one more outside with the ordinary people, the other more inside with the learned in their temples and then their successors – money gradually emancipated itself. But, in becoming something unto itself, it abandoned its true role in the economy and by the century's end, the separation of money and accounting had advanced so far that the resulting gap had to be overcome by the idea of business cycles.[28]

In addition, by the early 20th century, it had become impossible to conduct economic life on a basis of competing empires, a fact underlying the suspension of the gold standard as an

---

[28] Originating with H. L. Moore in the 19th century, the notion of the business cycle carries the message that economic events are not of man's making, but are as 'natural' as the cycle of the seasons. We can only follow them and are not, therefore, their authors. Needless to say, such a concept does not figure in associative economics.

instrument of economic equilibrium. By the end of the World War I, the great question had become: What comes next?

In 1922, in responding to precisely this question, Rudolf Steiner described[29] how balancing an economy which is becoming worldwide, and therefore closed, depends, on the differentiation and management of three kinds of money: that used for trade, that used for investments (saving and lending), and that which, representing surplus value, should be given away.[30]

In all this, it is important to notice how, despite the wars that continually ravage human relations, and despite humanity's many different spoken tongues, a common language – that of accounting – is gradually finding its place throughout the world. Contemporary with globalisation, the introduction of electronics brings the evolution story to a certain culmination. A large proportion of transactions are effected by a simple, worldwide set of electronic book-entries, valid throughout the world irrespective of the country, language

---

[29] *Economics*, op. cit., Lecture 12.

[30] See Chapter 15.

or culture of the economic partners. Cash is no longer the main method of payment. Money is becoming global bookkeeping. The world over, money and accounting are becoming one and the same thing. In this sense, we can begin to speak of accounting-money.

14 Money, accounting and the nervous system

When it is a question of illustrating money and its effects, it sometimes happens that the blood and its circulation are taken as an example. That we speak, for example, of liquid assets when referring to cash or money at the bank gives credibility to this comparison, as do all the aspects of economics linked to circulation. Nevertheless, although this analogy has merit from a certain point of view, it can mislead our understanding of the essential role that money plays in social life.

Blood is fundamentally a living liquid. The bearer of heat and oxygen, it courses out through the arteries with the vigour of a mountain stream, returning from the periphery with the fullness of a meandering river. This has nothing to do, however, with the nature of money – or its numerical equivalent, accounting – which, is to reflect values. This requires a link with consciousness, implying a certain distance, coolness and disinterest. In this sense, money is in fact the very antithesis of blood.

To give an image of money that better explains its nature and function, one should rather refer to the *nerves*. Here we have something that is probably more than a simple analogy, a connection we can deepen by looking at money or accounting as expressions of the social organism's neuro-sensory system.

Without entering into it too much, consider the resemblance of structure between money, accounting, and the brain. The brain, for example, reveals a certain symmetry between the left and right lobes, and it is well known that this duality underlies the very different natures of our thinking: left brain – verbal, logical thought; right brain – representational, intuitive, artistic thought. Accounting offers us a comparable symmetry with its income and expenditure statement, on the one hand, and its balance sheet, on the other, each giving a very different reflection of the reality from which they derive. Coinage tells the same story: tails shows a value, heads an image, often that of an authoritative person or device.

Being almost dead, the nerves regenerate only with difficulty, a peculiarity that extends to all the senses and goes along with their need to be transparent to the environment. Having no life of their own, they can better transmit the reality which lives around them, in the same way as a window serves its purpose only if it does not keep the light to itself. It is the same for money: in acquiring its own dynamic, it becomes something unto itself and is then unable to play its proper role as an organ for the perception of values in the economy – a problem already touched upon.[31] In this regard, given today's fusion of money and accounting, it falls to accounting to find a solution to this problem.

---

[31] See Chapter 8.

15 Three kinds of money

Money has no smell, but maybe it has colour, the hue of which changes according to the use we put it to. We think that 1 is always 1 wherever it occurs and wherever it goes. Could it be, however, that the value of 1 differs depending on whether it is used to buy something, whether it is invested, or whether it is given away? Not that it is worth more or less than 1, but that the economic consequences of these uses are so different as to necessitate differentiation between them.

What does this mean? Let us first try to distinguish these qualities of money: the value of 1 which I use to buy something derives from the product or service acquired through the transaction. Afterwards, I am indifferent to what becomes of the 1. What counts is the product or service which continues to accompany me. But the value of 1 which I lend is quite another matter. Its value derives from the borrower, reducing if he is a swindler, increasing if he is a bright and successful entrepreneur. In this case, my 1 stays connected to me in time. Whether implicit or explicit, a contract keeps track of every 1 lent until it is repaid.

And still another value belongs to the 1 given. For me, who gives it, it has no value any more. But for the one who receives it, it creates a freedom space. Turned to the future, it contains the potential of creativity, research, or novelty. 1 is not always 1, therefore. Its value and its effects differ according to the use made of it.

Now, in order to bring health to the global economy, we need to find a way to measure and thus to bring balance between these various kinds of money. How can they become visible and active principles in the world? The means to do so already exists: it is accounting. As used almost everywhere in the world today, accounting traces the circulation of values and in its very structure provides a clear means for apprehending the three kinds of money discussed here.

Let us take a closer look at this phenomenon. In what follows, the term 'business' is meant in its widest sense to include any initiative which produces accounts, that is, which is somehow linked to economic life. It can be a farm, a school, a factory, a doctor's practice, a government, or a bank. From an accounting point of view, it makes no difference.

The balance sheet is its first group of accounts. Its quality is that of a glance towards the business. Under 'assets'[32] it details the values which belong to the business – cash, inventory, what the customers have yet to pay, buildings, etc. Under 'liabilities'[33] it details the values which it owes to others – its borrowings, invoices yet to be paid, etc. Strangely also, liabilities includes owners' equity, a fact that can disarm the accounting novice. Yet does this not point to some unspoken wisdom? Even owners' equity – which is the financial base of the business – is, from an accounting point of view, lent to it by others. By keeping track of the past, the balance sheet shows the current state of the business. Every movement which has taken place is recorded there for ever; only a movement in the oppo-

---

[32] What it owns, the active side.

[33] What it owes, the passive side.

site direction and for the same amount can erase it.

Quite different is the quality of the second group of accounts, the income and expenditure statement. This looks away from towards the world (as is, indeed, shown in its counter-intuitive signage: + for expenditure, − for income) and describes the variations due to the many activities of the business. Under 'receipts', are detailed what the world paid for the things produced by the business, 'expenses' show what the world received from the business by way of the goods and services it bought. While the balance sheet measures a *state*, the income and expenditure account measures the *flow* of money coming in and going out. And, just like a physical meter, the income and expenditure statement has to be returned to zero from time to time. In contrast to the balance sheet, every movement which takes place in the income and expenditure statement is periodically erased.

This brings us to the third quality, that of the closing of the accounts. Here the view is of the business and the world at one and the same time. With the closing of accounts, the values on the balance sheet are adjusted, the income and expenditure statement is put to zero, and the result for the period – the surplus or deficit, profit or loss – appears. Whether positive or negative, at this stage the result loses its link with the income and expenditure statement and becomes freed from it, usually passing without thought or further ado onto the balance sheet. But to whom does it belong? A very special moment of consciousness permeates the closing. The meaning or raison d'être of the business, its partners, its natural and cultural environments, its place in the future of humanity, the way it meets human needs – all these things are reflected in the closing. But usually this question does not come into our consciousness and the business simply appropriates the result, transferring it to its balance sheet, where it melts into owners' equity (or its equivalent). And then it begins a new period.

With accounting-money,[34] we already have a differentiated instrument of perception which contains much more wisdom than we might notice at first sight. Only accounting-money allows us to see in a precise way the evolution

---

[34] One could also say 'money as bookkeeping'.

of money according to its three qualities, here matched to Steiner's nomenclature: purchase in the income and expenditure statement, loan money in the balance sheet, including owners' equity, and gift money in the surplus or deficit 'freed' by the closing of the accounts. The full significance of these crucial differences is not yet appreciated, however. Economics, in particular, balks at this means of reconnecting economic science with reality. And yet, all over the world, research is tending exactly in the direction of clarifying the relation between economic reality and its reflection in accounting.[35] The effort is underway to ensure that when, as it were, we look in the mirror of accounting, we all see the same thing.

Thus, accounting already gives us the possibility of differentiating the three kinds of money as they exist in the world today. And nothing stops us from beginning to use accounting as a means to assess the aptness of our decisions. For example, is it better to help a business by means of the balance sheet, that is, by lending, or to promote trade with it, that

---

[35] In this connection, see the recent work of the London-based International Accounting Standards Board (www.iasb.co.uk).

is, by means of the income and expenditure statement? Depending on where and how we use money, the result will be very different between one place and another and thus the general equilibrium also. Whether we act at the level of a simple group of companies, or of an 'institution' (such as a pension fund), or even of a whole country, this question is enough to enable us to perceive the importance, not only of the amount of money involved, but also and especially the type of money. It is on this new dimension that the equilibrium and coherence of the world economy will come to rest.

92

16 Budgeting and forecasting

To accompany the human being to the heart of economic life, we provided him with an appropriate instrument of perception: accounting-money. To the degree that he proves capable of perceiving the consequences of his deeds, he will become aware of his responsibilities also, and in that way become truly free.

At this stage, however, the meaning of perception must be widened. To understand it only as passive receptivity, as does a mechanical conception of the human being, is to miss altogether its essential nature. Perception is not only an activity; it is the source of all activity. Here we enter the deep mysterious world of the human will. Perception and willing invariably go together. If we could not perceive our movements, we would also be incapable of carrying them out. It is our perception that guides and adjusts every conscious movement towards its purpose.

In this way, we can understand why the new organ for perceiving the economy – accounting-money – is also the instrument of our economic activity, that which enables us consciously to lead our will towards its purpose in economic life.

In describing the structure of accounting-money, we have considered how its two sets of accounts – the balance sheet and the income and expenditure statement – receive the reflections of a past reality, so many footprints left in the sand. But this is only one aspect. Turned towards the future, the same organ is going to bring the awakening necessary if dreamy ideas linked to enthusiasm are to become realised. Accounting-money now becomes budgeting or forecasting. It throws light on the unknown that is to come and brings coherence and realism to the ideas and potentials that bubble up inside one.

This is why the initiator of any project is well advised to attend carefully to this task if he wants to realise his ideas, which otherwise could all too easily remain unfulfilled. Better then to budget or forecast; these are the means for making ideas happen.

Begin by dreaming… then courageously let

the imagination unfold freely to form a big picture of all one's ideas and hopes, but also the obstacles one can expect. Now, one by one, remove the colours and forms from the picture and allow values (in the form of figures), to come to expression in their stead. Such and such a month, such and such an objective, such and such a task, such and such an amount. Another month, another activity, another amount. And so on… until you obtain a satisfactory image made up of figures for a whole year, and even several. Finally, emboldened by this experience, commit your will to it and make it happen. The moment will then arrive when the first footprints (the actuals) will appear alongside the budget, confirming here what was anticipated and the road travelled, requiring there a change of course or an adaptation of the forecasts concerning the continuation of the activity.

Thus, the circle is closed.

This is to write large in economic life what happens, at the level of our bodies, with each conscious gesture. We outline the initial impulse, commit ourselves to realise it, then, on observing the result, learn to bring it about in a way that we can take responsibility for it.

Just as the human being depends on the nervous system which sinks into the depths of his limbs in order to be able to move his body, so he needs accounting-money to reflect the most unconscious areas of human relations in order to be able to move socially.

Through the organ of perception that accounting-money provides, the economy reveals a role more important by far than the one that we normally give it – that of meeting one another's needs. But not only in the outer, even sentimental, sense of producing what people really need, rather than what one needs to sell them in order to make a return to capital; but in a far deeper sense. The role of economic life is to light up the deep forces of human will and to enable them to act coherently with those of other human beings – in other words, bringing to light the destiny of each human being and then giving it the space to express itself in consonance with the destiny of others.

17 Association and regulation

Who has not had the experience of undertaking a shared project with one or several partners? For a long time, it is elaborated and discussed and the ideas all seem crystal clear. The roles are then shared out and each sets to work as best he knows how. But now the first surprises appear: what in thought expressed itself so clearly and agreeably can appear quite different when the will takes hold.

We have seen how an essential role of accounting-money is to accompany the delicate passage of thought into deed and to allow the human being to exercise freedom *and* responsibility. The same instrument becomes inescapable when it is a question of forming a durable economic association in the sense indicated in chapter 1.

First of all, it allows a climate of confidence to develop between the various partners, as we will see. Admittedly, to transcribe ideas into figures tends to reduce the mobility of the initial image. But this is so of any process of consciousness: the more consciousness grows, the more life escapes. Yet what results is permeated with a certain objectivity. What was hidden completely from the others in the intimate depths of the process which led from idea into action now comes to the surface. Shared with others, a transparency is added which becomes the foundation of mutual confidence.

Only there does the term association become reality. Personal egoism, previously all focused on itself, begins to widen. This is not a matter of moralising. What takes place is the direct consequence of increasing confidence: a gradual identification with the other, and the increasing interest which is inherently part of the experience. There are numerous examples. For some, the context will be the family, for others the amateur theatre group or the badminton club. All the environmentalist, Third-World, and feminist movements are expressions of such egoism extending beyond the limits of the individual person into their groupings, and then on into humanity as a whole. Now, we can help strengthen this awareness by the use of accounting-money.

After each participant in an association has formed his own accounting image, he can form with his colleagues a overall image which they represent collectively by showing one another their accounts in a fully transparent way. This extra step strengthens their experience of their combined economy, gradually attracting the attention of the others, their interest, and then their higher egoism. The whole then becomes as important as the parts.

We thereby arrive in the landscape of a new stage in economic development. Each contributes to the image of the whole and each can thereby perceive the consequences of his acts. But now we are not confronting one another: we are all in front of figures. Figures create a distance between the participants which allows them to avoid the mindless clashes that can arise when will forces are expressed too spontaneously. A real meeting can then come about. At once universal and unique, this meeting is without precedence for the regulation of economic life.

Universal… because the reality which ensues from it is the most objective one can imagine in economic life. No place of observation would better know how to serve as reference than that given by the meeting of the various points of view of the very protagonists, nor would any organ of perception better know how to reflect reality than that formed collectively by their own accounts. Whatever the situation – whether a meeting between consumers, distributors and producers, between entrepreneurs and investors or employees, between various partners in a business, or between different sectors or even countries themselves – the archetype remains the same: a meeting of those concerned around the reflected figure-version of their activities. Here we come to the heart of economic regulation: it is through *associating* that regulation will come true. To impose the external regulation of the markets in the name of more objectivity is to part company with reality, opening the door to the illusory regulation of market forces and the invisible hand. It amounts to an abdication of responsibility and thus a renouncement of freedom. Human beings must learn to do, together and consciously, what they otherwise leave to an external agency, in the false expectation that it can or will act on their behalf.

Unique... because every meeting has its specific character due to its particular economic situation in terms of scale and frequency, the people who compose it, and the rules of governance that they evolve and abide by. Everywhere, such meetings can make visible what is evolving in the depths of the economy – that is, in the will life of human beings – and thereby provide the means to balance out excesses and to guide the future.

In such a world, prices become the indicators of economic reality and the three kinds of money become the means to perceive evolution and to maintain coherence. If certain goods are too expensive, the association can act so that as a consequence their price can fall. If a certain service is no longer profitable, they can take appropriate measures so that its price can rise. Not that associations can act *directly* on prices – that is no more possible economically than one can lower the temperature in a room by moving the position of the needle or by pressing down on the column of mercury – but they engender the real conditions, which will lead to a change in prices in the way required.

It is associations such as these, that, through regular meetings taking place throughout the world, will allow us to become truly aware of the world economy and to regulate its development.

18 A money for the world

The economy today is a prisoner of false imagery. For almost a century, its natural tendency to be global has been held back within the limits of national borders. Wherein, though, lies the real problem? Not in the rules of protectionism, as free market proponents would have us believe, but in choosing and maintaining the conception of the nation-state with its own economy,[36] a fact that leads to wild competition between national currencies and prevents the next step.

The whole world is involved in the production of the smallest match, all kinds of food, tools or clothing. No meal, no activity, no leisure – let alone communications – is without a direct or indirect relation with the most distant parts of the planet. Seen from this angle, world economy is already a fact. However, the organs for perceiving it, and espe-

---

[36] See note on page 32.

cially those for managing it, are by no means yet established. In particular, we have neither global money nor global accounting.

Many sorts of instrument have indeed already been developed to help us trade effectively throughout the world and to facilitate transactions, payments and investments, regardless of the place of production or consumption. But, while these tools provide necessary services for a world economy, they do not allow the development of conscious regulation. Moreover, they have become themselves so many secondary markets with a perturbing effect on the entire world economy, not unlike that of pirates in former times.

In the 19th century, the economy balanced itself in a gradual way. If somewhere the price of a product fell, balance was restored by trade with neighbouring countries. However, the regulation inherent in the interaction of multiple economies is impossible once the economy becomes global and closed unto itself. It no longer has another economy through which to restore balance. It has to find in itself its source of coherence and stability.

As this book has discussed, this can be achieved through a *global accounting-money* that is (1) *independent* of all countries and (2) *consciously articulated into three kinds*.

These two conditions are essential.

The first condition guarantees the autonomy of the world economy with regard to nation-states and makes of every country a rights state only. It implies the dissolution of the nation-state and ends the need for protectionism. The creation of the euro in a part of Europe shows that global accounting-money is not only a wonderful idea, but one that is readily practicable.

The second condition gives at once a triple reference for monitoring the stability of the world economy. The example of the chaos now reigning in the world of pensions illustrates well how little attention was paid to the various kinds of money. None of the numerous comments which are in the forefront of current events approaches the problem from this point of view. Indeed, when, during the 1970s, the consequences for pensions of the pyramid of ages were realised, we got into our heads that it was enough for everyone to put aside sufficient money for his retirement to mitigate the problem. But we did not see that thereby money changed its nature and that this would have consequences. Purchase money (income and expenditure statement), was turned into loan money (balance sheet). When this mechanism of forced savings was introduced almost simultaneously into all the industrial nations, a large-scale imbalance became predictable.[37] Less money to be spent, more money to be invested, until there is too much money to be invested… then comes the inevitable crash, with every step undermining a little more the social tissue by increasing pressure on profitability. The aim was to ensure a better future, but we broke everything in the space of one single generation! And so we arrived at precisely the situation we were trying to avoid – the need to increase the age of retirement while decreasing the level of pensions.

To these two conditions, we need to add an implicit third: we need to be careful *not* to

---

[37] In 1985, when Swiss law made employee pensions obligatory, this problem, and possible ways to combat it, was already taken into account in the formation of CoOpera – Pension fund for artists and self-employed PUK, based in Ittigen, near Berne.

open the way through this to the creation of a world state.

The greatest threat to a healthy evolution towards a world economy comes once again mainly from the concept of nation-states. Instead of participating in the creation of a single currency, independent of countries and articulated consciously according to its three-fold nature, today's nation-states risk becoming trapped in a dead-end, characterised by the military assertion of separate currencies and requiring the creation of competing monetary blocs supported by media frenzy, political edicts, and acts of war.

The economy will not have become a world affair until it has been released from national monetary hindrances. This is its real challenge in the 21st century.

Over to me…

We have seen that the future of economic life is humanity's joint affair. The challenge is to bring more consciousness into our will, our actions. Then economic life will no longer be something done to us, but something we have willed together…

We are each first called to this task as *consumers*. When I buy something, am I attracted by the product, its origin, its quality and the way it answers my needs? Or am I just going for the lowest price, going miles out of my way to find the cheapest vendor, even though I pay for it in wasted time and petrol, even changing country in pursuit of better 'value'?

We are also called upon as *lenders* or *as investors*. When I have some spare money, which I am not going to need immediately, do I look for a project which corresponds to my values, looking around me to find entrepreneurs in whom I can place my confidence? Or do I entrust my savings to anonymous investment funds, which, like so many silent boomerangs, function beyond the control of human intervention?

Lastly, we are each called to act as *entrepreneurs,* carriers of initiative. As a director of a business or any other economic organisation, alone or with others, do I seek transparency and share my economic situation with others? Supported by accounts, do I regularly review and report my activities? Or do I consider the figures of my business to be mine alone, showing my accounts to myself only and acting *in camera*?

As we have seen, by allowing us to respond to one another's needs, the economy reveals to us the deep forces of our will and permits us to act coherently with that of others. We are the heart of the problem, and also its solution. Everything depends on our deeds.

In the words of Denis de Rougement, "The future is within us." If we would make it right, we only need the will to do so.

*I have discovered
the secret that after
climbing a great hill,
one only finds that
there are many more
hills to climb.*

Nelson Mandela

Appendix:
The mark of association

We have seen how the associative approach to economic life rests on the responsibility experienced by each human being in partnership with his circle of acquaintances and investors. Its objective is to develop the instruments that allow consciousness of this responsibility to grow and thereby gradually to regulate economic life, allowing us to move beyond competition and market forces.

As we saw, the first actors would be the consumers; each in this view is called on to make a start. The second actors would be the investors – there, though, the opportunities are already fewer and the choices more difficult. The third actors would be the entrepreneurs, all those who through their ideas and initiative give form to a project and assume responsibility for it.

In regard to the latter, a Quality Guarantee Mark has been created that captures the essential characteristics[38] of an associatively-run organisation.

Its stated purpose is 'to recognise and guarantee the associative economic quality of any organisation whether it is agricultural, industrial, commercial, financial, governmental, humanitarian or cultural, and regardless of its size, locality and domain of operation.'

Four criteria were initially registered, which reflect directly the ideas described in this book. They define the minimum conditions for speaking of an associatively-run organisation or business. They are but a point of departure, and need to be developed by the users of the Mark themselves in the light of their experiences and needs.

These criteria suppose an entrepreneur, an appropriate legal structure, transparent accounting, and a regular Meeting with other user-entrepreneurs:

---

[38] The following extracts are from the regulations governing the Mark, see www.ae-institute.com.

1. The human being is taken as the reference and point of departure :

'The responsibility and management of the Organisation is in the hands of a person or persons striving to understand associative economics…'

2. The legal form adopted by the organisation manages and distributes its power so as to permit the organisation to maintain coherence between its freedom and its responsibility, its decisions and its acts:

'The structure of the Organisation is such that its existence as a legal person, the management of its activities, and the financing of its means of production are distinguished from each other … so that no one element has undue power over the other two. In particular:

Its aim and existence are independent of both the providers of the finance for its means of production and of the views and opinions of its management,

Its financing of the means of production is designed to guarantee its long term independence,

Its management functions in a transparent manner and maintains a clear record of decisions taken.'

3. The accounts are open and transparent. They form the common language of communication between user-entrepreneurs and are the key to a responsible future:

'The accounting of the Organisation is open and transparent both internally and externally.

Based on double-entry bookkeeping, it is structured in terms of a universal framework defined by the Association to provide a common language for all Organisations.

Each Manager establishes a budget and maintains the bookkeeping and year-end forecasting for the Organisation (or the part of the Organisation) that he represents.

In the event of an Organisation having more than one Manager, the Managers together establish a budget and maintain the bookkeeping and year-end forecasts for their Organisation as a whole.

In the same way, a budget is established and the bookkeeping and year-end forecasting maintained for each group of Organisations that meets (see 4.4a below).'

4. Based on figures, the regular Meeting with other user-entrepreneurs, creates a space to report on their initiatives and thus to help make them objective:

'Independently of any trading or financial relationships, the Manager of an Organisation and the Managers of at least two other Organisations hold a meeting of constant composition and on regular basis at a frequency agreed with the Association – hereinafter

"the Meeting". The meeting will be a real one; that is, the Managers must be in the same room.

The purpose of the Meeting is for the Managers to share and comment on the economic situation of their respective Organisations through the medium of budgets, management accounts, and year-end forecasts, as a basis for building a shared picture of their own and each others' situations both individually and together.

The year-end is the occasion of a similar Meeting, at which the aims and budgetary options of the Organisations for the following year are likewise considered and made clear.'

In this way, the attempt has been made to give explicit shape – valid for the collaboration between several businesses or groups of businesses – to the axioms of an associative economy outlined in this book: *the human being* and *the legal person* whom he inevitably inhabits in becoming economically active, *the others* without whom no economy would be possible and *accounting-money* as the medium suited to their *meeting*.

The criteria describe but a first step, to be followed by others. The rules that accompany the Mark describe how this will be done through meetings of the users to develop the rules in a coherent and most effective way.

Associative Economics Institute Publications

A Human Response to Globalisation
Discovering Associative Economics
Marc Desaules
(Also in French)

The Metamorphosis of Capitalism
Realising Associative Economics
Christopher Houghton Budd

Step into Another World!
A Collaboration